CONTENTS

TRADITIONS

OF THE UNITED STATES SENATE

At a few yards' distance [from the Chamber of the House of Representatives] is the door of the Senate, which contains within a small space a large proportion of the celebrated men of America. Scarcely an individual is to be seen in it who has not had an active and illustrious career: the Senate is composed of eloquent advocates, distinguished generals, wise magistrates, and statesmen of note, whose arguments would do honor to the most remarkable parliamentary debates of Europe.

— Alexis de Tocqueville, *Democracy in America*, 1835

Welcome to the Senate of the United States, the "World's Greatest Deliberative Body." No one knows for certain who coined that phrase. It came into widespread use in the latter half of the 19th century, and many have questioned its accuracy at various times in the nation's history, but those words are routinely applied to no other legislature than the "upper house" of the United States Congress. Alexis de Tocqueville's influential 1830s survey of American government, published in the early years of the Senate's "Golden Age," helped to promote that notion.

The U.S. Senate relies heavily on tradition and precedent. Change comes slowly. Many of its current rules and procedures date from the First Congress in 1789. The major amendment to the U.S. Constitution affecting Senate operations—the 17th Amendment providing for direct popular election of its members—took 87 years from the time of its initial drafting in 1826 to its ratification in 1913. The decision to make it possible under the Senate rules to limit debate required 128 years of consideration. In conducting late 20th-century Senate impeachment trials, the Senate closely followed procedures established in the 1790s and updated in the 1860s. Senate officials still carry 18th-century titles such as "secretary," "clerk," "keeper of the stationery," and—until recently—"wagon-master."

Traditions of the United States Senate offers a guide to the distinguishing customs and rituals of the institution that Pulitzer Prize-winning author Allen Drury lovingly described as "this lively and appealing body."

Becoming a Senator

Orientation programs. Post-election orientation programs provide new members a foretaste of Senate traditions. Prior to 1976, beginning members looked to the other senator from their states, or to party officials, for advice on how to survive in this unfamiliar environment. Arizona Senator Barry Goldwater recalled how deeply he valued this assistance.

> *Early in January 1953, a very frightened and somewhat timid desert rat landed in Washington, feeling as out of place as anyone possibly could. I had not been in my hotel room 15 minutes when the phone rang and the voice at the other end said, "This is Mark Trice." I wondered then who that could be. He immediately told me that he was Secretary of the Senate and his interest that morning was in helping me to get started. He came to me like a life ring comes to a drowning man.*

Secretary of the Senate J. Mark Trice

The 1976 election produced 17 new members—the largest infusion in 18 years. The next two elections generated even larger classes, with 20 in 1978 and 18 in 1980. These three elections, along with the 1980 change in party control for the first time in 26 years, encouraged Senate officials to develop well-organized and responsive welcoming programs. (In years with smaller classes, such as 1990 with only four new members, the programs have necessarily been less formal.)

Typically, these programs cover several days in November or December and coincide with party leadership elections. Presenters range from the party floor leaders to veterans of the most recent previous freshman class. Sessions span a host of practical topics from "parliamentary procedure" and "setting up a new office," to "life in the Senate." In addition to this bipartisan, Senate-wide program, each of the two political parties organizes briefings and retreats.

In December 1996, Senate party leaders asked Senator Robert C. Byrd—who subsequently became the longest-serving member in Senate history—to brief new senators. At a closed meeting in the Senate Chamber, that 15-member class received the following advice, which was later published in the *Congressional Record.*

> *Service in this body is a supreme honor. It is also a burden and a serious responsibility. Members' lives become open for inspection and are used as examples for other citizens to emulate. A Senator must really be much more than hardworking, much more than conscientious, much more than dutiful. A Senator must reach for noble qualities—honor, total dedication, self-discipline, extreme selflessness, exemplary patriotism, sober judgment, and intellectual honesty. The Senate is more important than any one, or all, of us. . . . Each of us has a solemn responsibility to remember that, and to remember it often.*
>
> *The Senate and, therefore, Senators were intended to take the long view and to be able to resist, if need be, the passions of the*

often intemperate House. Few, if any, up-per chambers in the history of the western world have possessed the Senate's absolute right to unlimited debate and to amend and block legislation passed by a lower House. . . . [Its] deference to minority views sharply distinguishes the Senate from the ma-joritarian House of Representatives. The Framers recognized that a minority can be right and that a majority can be wrong.

The pressures on you will, at times, be enormous. . . . A Senator's attention to-day is fractured beyond belief. . . . But, somehow, amidst all the noise and con-fusion, you must find the time to reflect, to study, to read, and especially to un-derstand the absolutely critically impor-tant institutional role of the Senate.

The Senate is often soundly castigated for its inefficiency, but in fact, it was nev-er intended to be efficient. Its purpose was and is to examine, consider, protect, and be a totally independent source of wisdom and judgment on the actions of the lower house and on the executive. As such, the Senate is the central pillar of our Constitutional system. I hope that you, as new members, will study the Sen-ate in its institutional context, because that is the best way to understand your personal role as a United States Senator.

Oath taking. At the beginning of a new six-year term, before senators-elect can exercise their legislative responsibilities, each must take the prescribed oath of office in an open session of the Senate. From the earliest days, an elaborate tradition developed under which senators-elect—both freshmen and reelected veterans—are escorted down the Chamber's center aisle to take the oath from the presiding officer. Customarily, the other senator from the member-elect's state serves as escort.

Occasionally, the senator-elect chooses a member from another state. Former senators sometimes share these honors. In 2003, former Senator Bob Dole escorted his wife, Elizabeth Dole, to take her oath. In recent years, parents have proudly escorted their children in this ritual, with former Senators Frank Murkowski, Birch Bayh, and David Pryor shepherding, re-spectively, Senators Lisa Murkowski, Evan Bayh, and Mark Pryor.

Senators-elect affirm their oath to defend the U.S. Constitution by stepping forward, raising their right hand, and repeating the words spoken by the presiding officer. Some carry in their left hand a personal Bible or other sacred text.

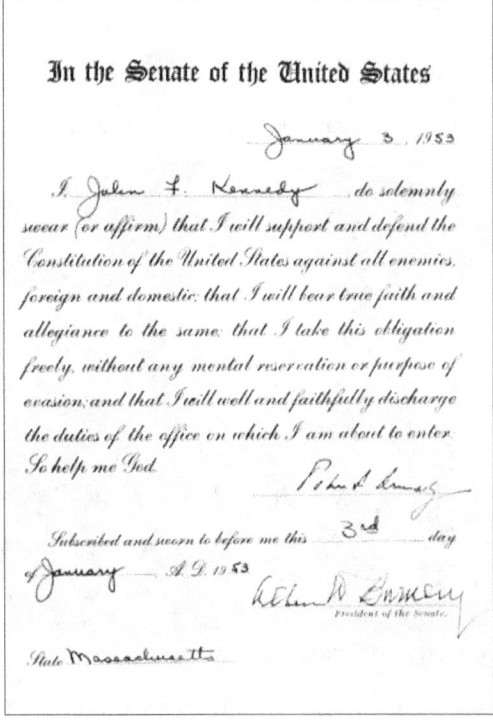

Senate Oath Book, January 3, 1953

The high point in the oath-taking ceremony occurs as the secretary of the Senate invites each newly sworn senator to sign his or her name on a specially dedicated page in an ornate oath book. This practice began during the Civil War, after the Senate adopted an 1864 rule requiring all senators to supplement their oral affirmation by signing a printed copy of a wartime loyalty oath. The so-called "Ironclad Test Oath" included a provision by which senators swore that they had never supported the nation's enemies—domestic or foreign. The Test Oath was designed to keep former Confederates from taking positions within the federal government after the war.

Until 1987, when the first Senate swearing-in ceremony was broadcast on live television, these events were off-limits to cameras of any sort. The longstanding ban on photography in the Senate Chamber led newly sworn members to devise an alternate way of capturing this moment for their families, constituents, and posterity. Prior to 1977, the vice president invited senators and their families into his formal Capitol office to reenact the ceremony for home-state photographers. When the remodeled Old Senate Chamber opened in 1976, reenactment ceremonies moved to that elegant setting, evoking the "Golden Age" of the mid-19th-century Senate.

Members' order-of-service numbers.

Another informal custom of opening-day proceedings is to advise newly sworn freshmen of their "number." New members' responses to this information range from confusion to curiosity. "What does my number mean?"

This tradition began in the late 1970s, when a senior senator asked the Senate Historical Office to calculate the number of senators who had served prior to 1959 and to compile a chronological list of all senators who had arrived since that year. This list displayed members' names arranged and numbered by their relative seniority at

the time of their initial oath-taking, beginning with Ohio Senator Stephen Young at number 1,572.

By tradition, the Senate determines seniority for the purpose of assigning office space according to former government service and then state population. The highest ranking goes to those with previous service, in descending order, as a senator, vice president, House member, cabinet secretary, and governor. For those with no service in these categories, seniority is calculated according to state population, from largest to smallest.

In 2000, the Historical Office extended this list back to the Senate's first meeting in 1789. Assigning numbers alphabetically within each arriving class, this list—available on the Senate Web site—designates Richard Bassett of Delaware as senator number one. During the 110th Congress, in June 2007, John Barrasso of Wyoming became senator number 1,896.

Senators of the First Congress

This custom symbolizes the continuous chain of membership from the Senate's founding era to the present. Some senators demonstrate particular pride in their assigned number. At least one displays it on his automobile's license plates.

"Father of the Senate." The extended Senate community of members, spouses, and staff is customarily likened to a family. Special deference is accorded to the elders of this unique family. Preeminent among these elders are committee chairs and ranking members, and the Senate president pro tempore. Formally and in countless casual ways, the president pro tempore emerged during the 20th century as the Senate's guiding father-figure. The constitutionally mandated official who presides over the Senate in the absence of the vice president, the president pro tempore since 1947 has been third in line of presidential succession behind the vice president and Speaker of the House. As the Chamber's presiding officer, the president pro tempore is authorized to perform certain duties including signing legislation before it is sent to the president, ruling on points of order, and enforcing decorum in the Senate Chamber. The natural development of a Senate "father" follows an Anglo-American tradition rooted in the practices of the United Kingdom's House of Commons. That chamber confers the formal title of "Father of the House" upon its most senior member, who presides at the election of a Speaker and on occasions "where historical perspective may be required."

In previous generations of senators, members have recognized as Senate "fathers" those individuals who became fervent defenders of the body's constitutional prerogatives and were well versed in the institution's history and customs. These paternal figures tended to emerge naturally from one era to the next. Two prominent 19th-century Senate "fathers" were Rhode Island's Henry Anthony and Massachusetts' George Hoar. In 1903, Senator Hoar summarized this role in describing Senator Anthony—whom the Senate had elected president pro tempore on 17 occasions.

He had come to be the depository of [the Senate's] traditions, customs and unwritten rules. . . . He seemed somehow the intimate friend of every man in the Senate, on both sides. Every one of his colleagues poured out his heart to him. It seemed that no eulogy or funeral was complete unless

Senator Henry Anthony, R–RI

Senator George Hoar, R–MA

Anthony had taken part in it, because he was reckoned [as a protecting] friend of the man who was dead.

In the mid-20th century, Senators Robert Taft of Ohio and Richard Russell of Georgia wore this mantle.

Seniority. The concept of a revered Senate "father" developed through the institution's first half century in tandem with the seniority principle. In its earliest decades, the Senate struggled to find an equitable means for distributing special status among members. Who would serve as president pro tempore in the absence of the vice president? Who would chair the important committees? Who would obtain desirable office space? Initially, the Senate conducted numerous and time-consuming roll-call votes to determine committee assignments. By the 1840s, a time of rapid membership turnover and short tenures in office, the Senate began recognizing seniority of service in arranging committee rosters. In 1858, however, the Senate briefly ignored seniority when its Democratic caucus removed Stephen Douglas as chairman of the significant Committee on Territories because he did not reflect that party's views on slavery. This departure from tradition—along with the 1871 removal of Charles Sumner as chairman of the Foreign Relations Committee for opposing an annexation treaty favored by the president—created hard feelings within the Chamber and banner headlines in papers across the nation. In later years, the Senate occasionally adjusted its committee seniority rules—most notably in 1997 when the Senate Republican Conference placed six-year term limits on its party's committee chairmen and ranking members.

Senate Bean Soup. No introduction to Senate traditions can be considered complete without sampling a steaming bowl of Senate Bean Soup. For more than a century, this appealing concoction has been available daily in all Senate dining areas. The origins of this venerable tradition are not entirely certain, but Minnesota Senator Knute Nelson first provided Senate chefs his favorite bean soup recipe in 1903. That recipe includes navy beans, hot water, smoked ham hocks, brazed onion, butter, salt, and pepper. In the 1970s, a popular Washington restaurant created its own "U.S. Senate Bean Soup," available in food stores in 15-ounce cans under the "Dominique's" label.

Senate Bean Soup being made

ON THE SENATE FLOOR

Senate officers. Senator Barry Goldwater's 1953 reference to the orientation assistance he received from Secretary of the Senate J. Mark Trice foreshadowed the full range of services offered to members—veteran and new—by the Senate's five elected officers. Those officers are the secretary of the Senate, the sergeant at arms, the two party secretaries, and the Senate chaplain. Today, incoming senators meet all five early in their formal orientation sessions.

In April 1789, shortly after achieving its first quorum, the Senate elected Samuel A. Otis as its secretary. A former speaker of the Massachusetts house of representatives and member of the Continental Congress, Otis helped in countless ways the First Senate's 26 members—all newly elected. He kept records of floor proceedings, disbursed payrolls, and purchased supplies. Today's secretary continues to provide the legislative, financial, and administrative support essential for the Senate to exercise its constitutional responsibilities and for senators to carry out their daily Chamber activities.

The sergeant at arms and doorkeeper, whose tenure also dates back to 1789, serves as the protocol and chief law enforcement officer of the Senate. This officer is responsible for escorting the president of the United States and other official guests of the Senate in the Capitol, and for maintaining security for members and facilities in the Capitol and Senate office buildings. The sergeant at arms is also responsible for all Senate computers and technology support services, recording and photographic services, printing and graphics services, and telecommunications services.

Senate desks. Incoming senators typically ask two questions related to their seating assignments in the Senate Chamber: "Which one of the 100 desks will I occupy?" and "Where will my desk be located?" In the Senate's earliest years, neither party nor seniority influenced members' seating locations. Available evidence suggests that senators chose to sit with friends or other members from their region. Tending to cluster by party affiliation from the 1840s, senators made the center aisle a clear boundary in 1877 when they began the practice of having desks shifted across that aisle following each election so that all members of a party could sit together.

By the late 19th century, Senate party leaders had come to rely on seniority to settle new members' questions about desk location. For decades after the Senate moved

Senate in session, 1877

to its current Chamber in 1859, members complained about that large, box-like room's poor acoustics. Its glass-paneled ceiling muffled most sounds, except those of pouring rain and beating hail. Determined to keep abreast of floor proceedings, many took the first opportunity, as desks became available, to move to better hearing locations toward the front and center of the Chamber. Only in 1971, following installation of the Senate's first effective voice amplification system, did acoustics no longer principally determine members' choices of desk locations. Fifteen years later, in 1986, the inauguration of gavel-to-gavel television coverage further influenced members' decisions about their preferred seating assignments. Today, some members continue to follow the historical pattern of moving toward the front and center as they gain seniority, while others settle on agreeable locations elsewhere in the Chamber.

While new members are limited in their choice of seat location, they may be able to negotiate for the assignment of a specific desk. Along with the original Senate gavel, the Chamber desks are the institution's most venerable relics. A New York cabinetmaker had fashioned 48 of them by 1819 to replace desks destroyed when invading British troops burned the Capitol in 1814. As new states entered the Union, the Senate commissioned additional desks. Today, reflecting early 19th-century senatorial needs, each desk includes an inkwell and a shaker that originally held finely ground fish bones, ideal for blotting ink newly applied to parchment and paper.

The Senate curator maintains a record of desk assignments—available on the Senate's Web site—with information dating from the earliest years of the 20th century. New senators often seek a desk previously associated with a respected home-state predecessor, a relative who may have preceded them in the Senate, or other illustrious former members. By special Senate resolution, desks of legendary members Daniel Webster, Henry Clay, and Jefferson Davis are assigned, respectively, to the senior senators from New Hampshire (Webster was born in New Hampshire, but represented Massachusetts in the Senate), Kentucky, and Mississippi. For senators interested in occupying a desk once assigned to an iconic figure within the Democratic party, there is a strong chance of obtaining a desk once used by Missouri Senator Harry S. Truman. The future president consecutively occupied 10 desks during his service from 1935 to 1945.

The task of compiling a roster of previous occupants has been made easier by the Senate tradition of inscribing the member's name in his or her desk drawers. Some have signed with pen and ink, while others have sought a more permanent medium, carving their names deeply into the supple wood. Sheets of Mylar now shield this unique historical record from potentially damaging contents within the drawers.

Drawer of Senate Chamber desk 43

Maiden speeches. When they are comfortable with their newly assigned desks, and have learned the protocol for casting recorded votes, new members consider the question, "When should I give my first floor speech?" In the mid-1950s, a Capitol Hill veteran offered this advice to newcomers: "There are two kinds of congressmen—show horses and work horses. If you want to get your name in the papers, be a show horse. If you want to gain the respect of your colleagues, keep quiet and be a work horse." From the Senate's earliest days, new members have observed a ritual of remaining silent during floor debates for a period of time—depending on the era and the senator. That period once ranged from several months to several years. Some reasoned that by deferring their so-called "maiden speech," their more senior colleagues would respect them for their evident willingness to serve an apprenticeship.

In 1906, Wisconsin Senator Robert La Follette had no intention of playing that role. He believed he had been elected to present a message for political reform that none of his more seasoned colleagues seemed inclined to deliver. Accordingly, the former governor, who was no stranger to the public spotlight, waited just three months before launching his first speech. That titanic oration consumed eight hours over three days and filled 148 closely printed pages of the *Congressional Record*. As La Follette began to speak, senators pointedly rose from their desks and left the Chamber.

Senator Robert M. La Follette, Sr., R–WI

Observing from the gallery, La Follette's disappointed wife interpreted this walkout as "a polite form of hazing."

In the 1950s, a freshmen senator complained about this tradition: "Like children, we should be seen and not heard." When a newly arrived senator of that day politely joined veteran members in lavish floor speeches honoring a senior member's birthday, the senior member privately criticized the upstart's temerity.

A decade later, freshman Senator Bob Dole considered three months of silence long enough. He chose April 14, 1969, for his first address. In that instance, he selected a personally important date—the 24th anniversary of the day he was wounded in Italy during World War II—to discuss challenges confronting disabled Americans. Following another ritual related to this first speech, he made a point every year, on or about April 14, of addressing that theme.

For most of the Senate's existence, the tradition of waiting several years before delivering a maiden speech has been much discussed but rarely observed. As one Senate insider explained, in this modern era of continuous and immediate news coverage, "the electorate wouldn't stand for it." Nonetheless, the tradition of paying attention to "maiden speeches," regardless of when they are delivered, remains important to senators, constituents, and home-state journalists.

Senate pages. New senators quickly learn to value the many helpful services of the Senate's pages. These services begin prior to the convening of each day's session. Pages place on each member's desk a copy of the *Congressional Record, Executive Calendar, Calendar of Business,* the day's pending legislation (both the bills and committee reports), legislative notices or bulletins, and—replacing the once traditional quill pens—two sharpened pencils. During the day, senators call on pages to send legislation to the presiding officer's desk, bring a glass of water, and carry out countless other errands. Today's pages are broadly representative of the nations's population of high school juniors from which they are selected. This was not always the case.

On April 15, 1965, less than a year after passage of the 1964 Civil Rights Act, New York Senator Jacob Javits made history by appointing the first African American Senate page, Lawrence Bradford, Jr. Six years later, on May 14, 1971, Senator Javits and Illinois Senator Charles Percy appointed the first two female pages, Paulette Desell and Ellen McConnell.

Senators Charles Percy and Jacob Javits with first female Senate pages

Senator Daniel Webster had selected the first Senate page in 1829. Proving that personal connections counted in those days, he chose nine-year-old Grafton Hanson, grandson of the Senate sergeant at arms. Two years later, the Senate added a second page, Isaac Bassett, the 12-year-old son of a Senate messenger.

Beginning a tradition in which service as a page sometimes became the first step on a

Senate career path, Grafton Hanson held a series of increasingly responsible Chamber jobs over the next 10 years. Isaac Bassett, who is well known to students of the institution's 19th-century folklore, remained in the Senate's employ for the rest of his long life. In 1861, he became assistant doorkeeper—a post in which he earned the legendary distinction of being the official who stopped a Massachusetts soldier from bayoneting the Senate desk previously occupied by Mississippi Senator Jefferson Davis, who had just become president of the Confederacy. Late 19th-century photographs show Bassett, by then an elderly man in a long white beard, exercising another tradition—one that has not survived to modern times. As the Senate hurried to wrap up end-of-session legislation, Bassett employed a long pole to move the Chamber clock's minute hand backwards from the twelve o'clock adjournment time to gain a few precious minutes.

Doorkeeper Isaac Bassett adjusts Senate Chamber clock

By the 1870s, the Senate required pages to be at least 12 years old, but no older than 16, although it occasionally ignored those limits. Until the early 1900s, pages were responsible for arranging their formal schooling during Senate recesses. In various page memoirs, there runs a common theme that no classroom could have offered an educational experience comparable to what they enjoyed on the floor of the Senate. At Vice President Thomas Marshall's

1919 Christmas dinner for pages, 17-year-old Mark Trice explained, "a Senate page studying history and shorthand has a better opportunity than a schoolboy of learning the same subjects, because we are constantly in touch with both. We boys have an opportunity to watch the official reporters write shorthand and they will always answer questions that we do not understand, thereby making a teacher almost useless." By May 1971, long after the Senate had established a professionally staffed page school, with the arrival of Pages Desell and McConnell, "we boys," had finally become, "we boys *and* girls."

Official photograph. In their first term, new senators join their colleagues for a group photograph, seated at their desks in the Senate Chamber. A Senate rule forbids "the taking of pictures of any kind" in the Chamber and surrounding rooms. In 1963, the Senate waived this rule for the National Geographic Society so that it could create the first formal portrait of the body in session for use in an illustrated guidebook on Congress. The Society's photographers next captured the Senate in 1971 and again in 1975. These three photos, taken from the rear of the Chamber, document an interesting evolution. The 1963 image shows senators sitting stiffly at their desks facing the presiding officer. In the 1971 picture, some members are slyly observing the photographer. By 1975, the entire Senate, perhaps more media savvy, is turned to fully embrace the camera. The Senate now poses once during each Congress for this traditional photo. It is the one regular occasion during any session in which all members are seated at their desks—and smiling.

First official Senate photograph, 1963

Senate of the 109th Congress, 2006

Candy desk. In traveling from a Senate office building to the Capitol, most senators enter the Senate Chamber through its eastern door, adjacent to elevators leading from the Senate subway. Just inside this door, to the right, along the aisle at the rear row on the Republican side, sits the "candy desk." This conveniently located fixture serves as a gathering spot for senators wishing to satisfy a late-afternoon energy deficit. California Senator George Murphy began this tradition more than 40 years ago. Soon after he entered the Senate in 1965, the former Hollywood actor and film executive began stocking his Chamber desk with candy to gratify his sweet tooth. In 1968, he moved to an aisle desk on the last row near the elevator entrance. Given the member traffic that regularly passed by his

new location, he invited other senators to help themselves and soon his desk became known to all as the "candy desk." After Murphy left the Senate in 1971, other sena-

Candy desk

tors who occupied the desk at that location carried on the tradition of keeping it well stocked with assorted mints, hard candies, and chocolates. Some senators asked for specific brands of candies and contributed funds for their replenishment. Various home-state candy companies have been happy to donate supplies. Given the candy desk's last-row location, its custodians have typically been members in their freshman term, including John McCain, Slade Gorton, Robert Bennett, and Rick Santorum.

Seersucker Thursday. In the years before air conditioning made summertime Washington bearable, senators from the South had much to teach their colleagues from other regions about proper attire. As spring merged into summer, southern senators shed their heavy-wool black frock coats for lighter linen and cotton garments. In 1907, a New Orleans clothier made summer wear more comfortable by designing a light-weight suit in pale blue and white striped rumpled cotton fabric. He named that fabric "seersucker," from Persian words meaning "milk and sugar." Seersucker suits became widely popular because they retained their fashionable good looks despite the frequent washing that humid summers made necessary.

Senatorial garb, from men's Victorian swallowtail coats to women's modern-era pantsuits, has regularly attracted media attention. Well into the 20th century, on the first warm days of spring, journalists routinely filed stories on the seasonal transformation evident in the poorly ventilated Senate Chamber. By the 1950s, however, modern air-conditioning had finally reached the capital city's interior spaces, making for year-round comfort—and year-round congressional sessions.

Seersucker Thursday, 2006

In the late 1990s, Mississippi Senator Trent Lott decided the time had come to revive a long-forgotten Senate sartorial tradition. He selected a "nice and warm" day in the second or third week of June to be designated Seersucker Thursday. His goal was to show that "the Senate isn't just a bunch of dour folks wearing dark suits and—in the case of men—red or blue ties." On the day before each year's event, senators are alerted to the impending "wearing of the seersucker." In 2004, California Senator Dianne Feinstein decided to encourage participation by the growing cadre of the Senate's women members. "I would watch the men preening in the Senate," she said, "and I figured we should give them a little bit of a horse race." The following year, 11 of the 14 women senators appeared on Seersucker Thursday in outfits received as gifts from Senator Feinstein.

Today, senators voluntarily make this annual fashion statement in a spirit of good-humored harmony to remind their colleagues of what earlier Senates considered mandatory summer attire.

SENATE FLOOR PROCEEDINGS

Chaplain's prayer. One of the Senate's most enduring traditions is the chaplain's daily prayer. Soon after the Senate first convened in New York City in April 1789, it selected the local Episcopal bishop as its chaplain. Moving to Philadelphia the following year, senators again chose that city's Episcopal bishop. Arriving in Washington, D.C., in 1800, the Senate continued selecting clergymen from mainline Protestant denominations—usually Episcopalians or Presbyterians—to deliver opening prayers and to preside at funer-

Senate chaplain delivers opening prayer, 1939

als and memorial services for departed members. These chaplains typically served for less than a year and conducted their Senate duties along with their responsibilities as full-time leaders of nearby parishes. In 1914, the Senate began including the full text of its chaplain's prayer in the *Congressional Record*.

Since the mid-20th century, the Senate has continued to draw its chaplains from the leading Protestant denominations, but the post has become a full-time assignment, with its incumbents tending to serve for a decade or more. Sensitive to the increasing religious diversity of the nation, the Senate invites representatives of other faiths as guest chaplains.

The chaplain reinforces the notion of the Senate—its members and staff—as an extended "family." When a Senate "family member" suffers the death of a loved one, or rejoices in the birth of a child, the chaplain may add an appropriate reference to the daily prayer. The chaplain also provides full-time pastoral care to members of the Senate community.

Pledge of Allegiance. Following the chaplain's prayer, the presiding officer leads the Senate in the Pledge of Allegiance.

The American flag had become a standard fixture in the Senate Chamber by the 1930s, placed directly behind the presiding officer. A half century later, as the Senate began televised coverage of its floor proceedings, the flag was moved to the presiding officer's right side so as not to appear to be bisecting that official's head on television screens. To balance the American flag, the Senate created a flag of its own—displaying the Senate seal on a field of dark blue—and placed it to the presiding officer's left.

Congress formally recognized the Pledge of Allegiance—first written in 1892—on December 28, 1945. In 1999, a New Hampshire resident contacted the office of Senator Robert Smith to inquire why the Senate did not follow the House, which had incorporated the Pledge into its proceedings 11 years earlier. Spurred by this inquiry, the Senate amended its standing rules on June 23, 1999, providing for the presiding officer to lead the body in the Pledge at the start of each daily session. President pro tempore Strom Thurmond inaugurated this tradition on the following day.

Senate gavels. The Senate lacks a specific symbol of its institutional authority comparable to the large ceremonial mace employed by the House of Representatives. In its place, a small ivory gavel conveys a sense of continuity and the importance of order in Senate proceedings.

At the start of each daily session, a Senate page carries a mahogany box with a hinged glass top into the Chamber and places it on the presiding officer's desk. The box, which remains on that desk whenever the Senate is in session, contains

Senate gavels, old and new

two hour-glass-shaped solid ivory gavels, each two-and-one-half-inches high. The older gavel had been in use at least since the 1830s, but had begun to deteriorate by the 1940s. In 1954, during a heated, late-night debate, Vice President Richard Nixon pounded the weakened gavel so vigorously that it splintered. Later that year, the government of India presented the Senate with a replacement, duplicating the original object with the addition of a floral band carved around its center.

When the Chamber becomes noisy, any member may request the presiding officer to suspend proceedings and restore order with a muscular pounding of this "ivory hammer." In 1866, Senator Charles Sumner praised former President pro tempore Solomon Foot for his skill as presiding officer.

His presence [at the desk] was felt instantly. It filled this Chamber from floor to gallery. It attached itself to everything that was done. Order was enforced with no timorous authority. If disturbance came from the gallery, how promptly he launched his fulmination. If it came from the floor, you have often seen him throw himself back, and then with voice of lordship, as if all the Senate was in him, insist that debate should be suspended until order was restored. "The Senate must come to order," he exclaimed; and meanwhile, like the god Thor, he beat his ivory hammer, in unison with his voice, until the reverberations rattled like thunder in the mountains.

Decorum. In his insistence on proper decorum, President pro tempore Foot followed the generations of Senate presiding officers who relied on Vice President Thomas Jefferson's 1801 *Manual of Parliamentary Practice for the Use of the Senate of the United States*. Reflecting cen-

President pro tempore Solomon Foot, R–VT

turies of contentiousness in legislative assemblies, Jefferson's *Manual* warned: "No one is to disturb another in his speech by hissing, coughing, spitting, speaking or whispering to another, nor to stand up or interrupt him, nor to pass between the Speaker and the speaking member, nor to go across the house, or walk up and down it, or take books or papers from the table, or write there." Earlier, Jefferson had drafted the rules of the Continental Congress, which the Senate followed closely in shaping its own rules in 1789. At least half of those 20 rules addressed issues of order and decorum.

Traditions of proper decorum developed naturally in the early Senate, which first got down to business with only 12 members present. Even into its mid-19th-century "Golden Age," with allowances for frequent absences, seldom were there more than several dozen members on the floor of the intimate, theater-like Old Senate Chamber. This contrasted with the noise and chaos of the cavernous House Chamber where more than 200 spirited members competed to hear and be heard. To ensure its ability to conduct proceedings without distractions or interruptions, the

Senate enhanced its sergeant at arms' authority to carry out the presiding officer's commands for decorum on the floor and in the galleries.

Early in the 20th century, the Senate added an important decorum-related rule. During 1902 floor proceedings, a senator openly questioned a colleague's integrity. When that colleague stormed into the Chamber to brand the assertion "a willful, malicious, and deliberate lie," the accusing senator jumped from behind his desk and punched his challenger in the face. Efforts to separate the combatants sparked a brawl. After the galleries were cleared and order restored, the Senate temporarily suspended both members from serving, censured them, and adopted stricter decorum guidelines for floor debate. Today's Rule XIX includes those 1902 guidelines: "No Senator in debate shall directly or indirectly, by any form of words impute to another Senator or to other Senators any conduct or motive unworthy or unbecoming a Senator."

Several years later, in 1914, the Senate ended two of its longstanding traditions in the interest of promoting decorum within the Chamber. It had been customary on the first day of a new session for senators to receive flowers at their desks from various admirers. (Some less popular members were suspected of sending bouquets to themselves.) When floral arrangements became so ostentatious that they blocked the aisles and obscured senators from public view, the Senate banned them from the Chamber—except in tribute following the death of an incumbent senator. In another move, owing to concerns about the respiratory problems of an elderly member, the Senate also banned smoking. (The dipping of snuff, however, continued for another half century. Two small lacquered boxes affixed to marble ledges adjacent to the presiding officer's desk offered a continuously replenished supply of that commonly used tobacco product, with several dozen spittoons conveniently placed throughout the Chamber. Today, these Senate relics are no longer in service, but they remain on view under protective boxes as a reminder of a once-famed Senate tradition.)

More than two centuries ago, Vice President Aaron Burr memorably extolled the Senate Chamber as a sacred place for deliberation. In his 1805 farewell address to the Senate, he described the room—and the institution—as "a sanctuary; a citadel of law, of order, and of liberty." In keeping with the tradition of its meeting place as a sanctuary, the Senate has turned aside requests to allow cell phones and laptop computers into the Chamber on grounds that they would interfere with its decorum.

"Golden Gavel" Award. Senior members typically advise new senators that the best way to learn about Senate floor procedure and decorum is to spend a significant amount of time in the Senate Chamber. For majority-party freshmen, this means taking a turn as temporary presiding officer. Until the 1950s, there was little opportunity for such on-the-job training because vice presidents of the United States regularly presided over the

Senate snuff box

Senate—the only duty that the Constitution assigns to that office. This changed in 1953. When Richard Nixon became vice president, he shifted his day-to-day focus to activities within the executive branch. Since then, vice presidents have appeared in the Senate Chamber principally when their vote is needed to break an anticipated tie, or for ceremonial functions. Over the past half century, the presiding officer's duties have fallen to the president pro tempore. As a senior senator of the majority party, presidents pro tempore chair a major committee and have other pressing duties that limit the amount of time available for presiding over the Senate. In the absence of that senior official, especially during long periods of routine proceedings when speech-making takes priority over bill-passing, the two party secretaries maintain a roster of junior members willing to preside in one-hour shifts. In 1977, the majority party determined that only majority party members would preside. (In 2001, when the Senate was evenly divided for several months, both parties briefly returned to the practice of furnishing presiding officers.)

In the late 1960s, to encourage freshmen senators to preside and learn Senate rules and procedures, the Senate majority leader created the Golden Gavel Award to acknowledge those who take the chair for a combined total of 100 hours during any year. The award now consists of a heavy brass, gold-plated gavel displayed in an attractive leather-covered box featuring an engraved plaque and the Senate seal. Some freshmen senators have so enjoyed this early mark of distinction that they sit for additional 100-hour periods, taking home multiple gavels. On February 12, 1999, at the conclusion of a five-week impeachment trial, the Senate presented an honorary Golden Gavel Award to Chief Justice of the United States William Rehnquist in gratitude for the time he spent presiding over that proceeding.

Senate President pro tempore James Eastland (center left) presents Golden Gavel Award to Senator Jesse Helms (right). Majority Leader Mike Mansfield (left) and Republican Leader Hugh Scott (center right) share in the festivities, 1973

Floor leaders' right of priority recognition. In the midst of heated legislative proceedings, freshmen members, seeking to catch the eye of the presiding officer so that they might be allowed to address the Senate, have reason to envy a privilege accorded only to the Senate's two floor leaders. At the opening of the 75th Congress, on January 5, 1937, Senate Republican Leader Charles McNary anticipated a difficult session. The 1936 congressional elections had produced a Senate with the lopsided party ratio of 76 Democrats to 16 Republicans. On that first day, McNary counted only one advantage—minor though it may have seemed at the time. He had become the first Republican floor leader to occupy a front-row, center-aisle seat in the Senate Chamber.

Until the early 20th century, the Senate operated without majority and minority leaders. In 1885, political scientist Woodrow Wilson wrote, "No one is the Senator. No one may speak for his party as well as for himself; no one exercises the special trust of acknowledged leadership." In the Senate's earliest decades, chairmen of major committees set the Chamber's agenda. The modern system of Senate party leadership emerged slowly in the years from the 1880s to the 1910s. During that period, both parties organized formal caucuses and selected conference chairmen who began to assume many of the roles of the modern floor leader.

Struggles with increasingly powerful presidents, the crisis of World War I, and the battle over U.S. entry to the League of Nations spurred the further evolution of Senate floor leadership. While party caucuses began to formally designate their floor leaders, they gave little thought to their placement in the Senate Chamber. If the leaders had desired to claim the front-row, center-aisle desks that have become the modern symbol of their special status, the presence of senior members comfortably lodged in those places dashed their hopes.

Finally, in 1927, the senior member who had occupied the prime desk on the Democratic side retired and party leader Joseph Robinson quickly took possession. Republican leaders had to wait another decade, however, before retirement opened up the corresponding seat on their side.

Later in 1937, Vice President John Nance Garner, a former Speaker of the House who valued leadership prerogatives, announced a new policy. Under the Senate rule requiring the presiding officer to "recognize the Senator who shall first address him," Garner established the precedent of giving priority recognition to the majority leader and then to the minority leader before all other senators seeking to speak. These two 1937 developments—priority recognition and front-row seating—contributed greatly to the evolution of modern Senate floor leadership.

Honoring distinguished visitors. The highest tribute the Senate can accord to a distinguished visitor is to announce the presence of that guest in open session and then briefly recess its formal floor proceedings so that senators may extend personal greetings. This honor is generally conferred upon foreign heads of state and parliamentary leaders. A variation on this procedure is for the Senate to proceed as a body to the Hall of the House of Representatives to attend a joint meeting of Congress to hear remarks by heads of state and prime ministers of nations whose good will is particularly important to the United States. Congress also convenes joint meetings to honor national heroes and to celebrate special anniversaries. Joint *meetings* of Congress are purely ceremonial in scope and are distinguished from joint *sessions,* which are sanctioned by the Constitution for delivery of the president's annual State of the Union address and for the quadrennial counting of presidential and vice presidential electoral votes.

British Prime Minister Winston Churchill addresses a joint meeting of Congress in the Senate Chamber, December 26, 1941

The first Senate reception for a distinguished foreign visitor took place on December 9, 1824, to honor the Marquis de Lafayette for his services to the cause of the American Revolution. Several days earlier, a joint Senate-House committee on arrangements had failed to agree on a common program for this occasion and decided to leave it up to each body to plan its own activities. The Marquis entered the Senate Chamber to the announcement, "We introduce General Lafayette to the Senate of the United States." He was seated at the dais next to the presiding officer, who then adjourned the Senate so that members could pay their respects. According to the record of that day's proceedings, the Marquis "cordially and feelingly reciprocated" those expressions. On the following day, the House received the Frenchman in its Chamber. That body's Speaker belatedly invited the Senate, which could not formally respond because it had adjourned for the weekend. Despite this, a number of senators attended and sat in specially reserved chairs, making this, in effect, the first joint meeting of Congress.

Many parliamentary bodies include formal processions among their highest rituals. The only such procession of the Senate takes place when it proceeds to the House for constitutional joint sessions and informal joint meetings. In this traditional rite, the secretary of the Senate and the sergeant at arms lead the way for the Senate president, or president pro tempore, followed by a double column of senators as they move from their Chamber through the Capitol Rotunda and Statuary Hall to the House Chamber. There they are conducted to reserved seats. In an exception to the southward direction of this procession, House members marched north to the Senate Chamber on December 26, 1941, less than three weeks after the U.S. entered World War II, to receive an ad-

dress from British Prime Minister Winston Churchill. With many members away for the Christmas holidays, congressional officials chose the smaller Senate Chamber to ensure their guest would be honored with a full audience. Since then, improved air transportation and the need for closer personal communication among the world's leaders and lawmakers have significantly increased the frequency of joint meetings.

Presentation of messages. The Senate regularly receives messages from the president of the United States and the House of Representatives. When a messenger enters the Chamber at the rear of the center aisle facing the presiding officer, that officer suspends the proceedings to recognize the emissary, who hands the message to a Senate aide, and departs.

When the Senate first convened in 1789, it spent considerable emotional energy on protocol issues. Driving the Senate's concern was a desire to ensure its equal—if not perhaps superior—status relative to the House. This was evident in the Senate's plan for delivering messages and legislation between the two chambers. The Senate considered its secretary a suitable envoy to the House. For House-passed legislation, however, the Senate desired that two members of that lower chamber serve as messengers. The House laughed at the Senate's proposal and instituted the tradition—parallel to that of the Senate—of sending all items under the supervision of an elected officer.

SENATE LEGACIES
Naming of buildings and rooms. On receiving their office assignments, new senators publicize their postal and e-mail addresses to encourage communication with constituents. Long before e-mail guaranteed citizens instantaneous access to their representatives in

Senator Richard Russell, D–GA

Senator Everett Dirksen, R–IL

Senator Philip Hart, D–MI

Washington, Senator Harry Truman jokingly informed his Missouri constituents that they could easily reach him at the following simple address: "Truman, S.O.B., Washington." Even as an obscure first-year senator in 1935, Truman knew the post office would direct any envelope marked S.O.B. to a member of the United States Senate.

That abbreviation for "Senate Office Building" served nicely until 1958, when a second facility opened. After that,

Harry S. Truman, D–MO, in his Senate office

senators had to specify in their addresses whether they resided in the "Old S.O.B." or "New S.O.B." Fourteen years later, in October 1972, the Senate provided for a third structure. This would eventually require each building to have a distinctive name. The old and new buildings, designated to honor two recently deceased Senate leaders, became the Richard Russell and the Everett Dirksen Buildings, respectively. In 1976, shortly after ground-breaking for the third building, the Senate named it for Michigan's then terminally ill senior senator, the widely admired Philip Hart.

The practice of honoring particularly distinguished members on the Senate side of Capitol Hill had begun two decades earlier, in 1955, with the naming of a new bell tower for the late Republican Majority Leader Robert Taft. That same year, the Senate set up a committee, chaired by Massachusetts Senator John F. Kennedy, to select five outstanding former members, whose portraits would be permanently displayed in the Senate Reception Room. In 1964, the Senate provided for the placement of plaques in adjacent Capitol rooms assigned to the two senators who formed the 1960 Democratic presidential ticket—John F. Kennedy and Lyndon B. Johnson.

Since then, other Capitol spaces have acquired designations associated with former Senate leaders. They include Arthur Vandenberg, Styles Bridges, Hugh Scott, Mike Mansfield, Robert C. Byrd, Strom Thurmond, Howard Baker, and Bob Dole. In 1998, plaques were installed in the original "S.O.B." to mark rooms once assigned to senators who subsequently became presidents of the United States: Warren Harding, Harry S. Truman, John Kennedy, Lyndon Johnson, and Richard Nixon.

Vice-presidential busts. Day and night, throughout the year, 20 grim-faced men keep watch over the Senate Chamber. Stationed in the gallery, they never speak. A gallery visitor might ask who they are and how they got there.

These silent sentinels memorialize individuals who held the office of vice president of the United States between 1789 and 1885. They got to their gallery niches because the Senate agreed on May 13,

Vice President Henry Wilson

1886, to commission marble portrait busts to note their service as presidents of the Senate. The career of Massachusetts Republican Henry Wilson inspired this plan. A popular senator and vice president, Wilson had died 11 years earlier in the Vice President's Room, near the Senate Chamber. To honor Wilson's memory, the Senate in 1885 engaged noted American sculptor Daniel Chester French, also of Massachusetts, to capture his image in marble. The Wilson bust is on permanent display in the Vice President's Room.

Daniel French subsequently assisted the Senate in establishing guidelines for the larger collection and agreed to prepare its initial entry—a likeness of his home-state hero and the nation's first vice president—John Adams. French accepted the Adams commission despite his misgivings about the paltry $800 fee the Senate had set for each work. "I consider it an honor and worth a great deal to have a bust of mine in so important a position," he said. "I do not know how many sculptors you will find who will look at it in the same way."

The Senate unveiled the portrait busts of John Adams and Thomas Jefferson on its 100th anniversary in 1889. By 1898, with all 20 of the gallery's niches occupied, additional busts took up positions in adjacent hallways. Today, each former vice president, from the late 18th century to modern times, occupies a place in this special pantheon. Inside the Chamber, Tennessee's Andrew Johnson will forever share a corner with Kentucky's John Breckinridge, whom he supported in 1860 for the presidency, denounced in 1863 for his military attacks on Tennessee, and pardoned in 1868 for his service as Confederate secretary of war. Outside, two of the Senate's best storytellers—John Nance Garner and Alben Barkley—flank the

Chamber's south entrance. Several paces to the right, Lyndon Johnson looks directly at Richard Nixon, the political adversary who followed him to the White House.

Senate Reception Room's "Famous Nine." In 1955, Senate Majority Leader Lyndon Johnson decided that all senators, including freshmen members, needed a "history lesson" to inspire pride in the contributions of their predecessors. At the request of Johnson and Republican Leader William Knowland, the Senate formed a special committee to identify five outstanding former members, no longer living, whose likenesses would be placed in vacant portrait spaces in the Reception Room, adjacent to the Senate Chamber. Leading the five-member committee was a 38-year-old freshman who had

recently written a book about courageous senators. Published in January 1956 under the title *Profiles In Courage,* that book earned Senator John F. Kennedy the 1957 Pulitzer Prize in biography.

The Kennedy Committee struggled to define "senatorial greatness." Should its members apply a test of "legislative accomplishment"? Perhaps, in addition to positive achievement, there should be recognition of—as they put it—"courageous negation." What about those senators who consistently failed to secure major legislation, but in failing, opened the road to success for a later generation? Personal integrity? That might exclude the chronically indebted Daniel Webster. National leadership? That would knock out great regional leaders like John C. Calhoun.

Reception Room unveiling, 1959

The unanimous respect of one's colleagues? That would doom the antislavery leader Charles Sumner.

The committee's established criteria nicely evaded these questions. It agreed to judge candidates "for acts of statesmanship transcending party and State lines" and to define "statesmanship" to include "leadership in national thought and constitutional interpretation as well as legislation." The committee further agreed that it would not recommend a candidate unless the vote was unanimous.

An advisory panel of 160 scholars offered 65 candidates. Sixty-five names for five spaces! Senator Kennedy quipped that sports writers choosing entrants to the Baseball Hall of Fame had it easy by comparison. As its top choice, the scholars' committee named Nebraska's Progressive Republican George Norris, a senator from 1913 to 1943. Senate panel member Styles Bridges, who had served with Norris from the late 1930s, harbored ill feelings from that association and consequently vetoed his consideration.

On May 1, 1957, the Kennedy Committee reported to the Senate its choices: Henry Clay of Kentucky, John C. Calhoun of South Carolina, Daniel Webster of Massachusetts, Robert Taft of Ohio, and Robert La Follette, Sr., of Wisconsin. In 2004, the Senate added two more outstanding former members, both of whom had flourished in the 1930s and 1940s. Republicans chose Arthur Vandenberg of Michigan and Democrats selected Robert Wagner of New York. In 2006, Senate leaders unveiled a portrait honoring Roger Sherman and Oliver Ellsworth, both of Connecticut, for their role in framing the compromise at the 1787 Constitutional Convention that established the basis of representation for the two houses of Congress. Sherman and

Ellsworth subsequently became distinguished late 18th-century senators. What is the traditional definition of senatorial effectiveness? Each of these nine senators offers a worthy guide.

Old Senate Chamber. New senators first visit the elegantly restored Old Senate Chamber as part of their post-election orientation program. They return weeks later, following their formal swearing-in ceremony, for a reenactment to satisfy home-state media "photo opportunity" requests. Over the course of a six-year term, members will likely revisit that place for events such as the unveiling of former Senate leaders' portraits, and for special programs associated with Senate history and culture.

This "noble room," as Henry Clay called it, housed the Senate from 1819 to 1859, as the body's membership grew from 42 to 64. Those four decades produced changes in the Senate's operations more profound than at any other comparable period in its history. In its so-called "Golden Age of Oratory," the upper chamber became the principal forum for national debates over westward expansion, economic development, and the abolition of slavery. The Senate emerged from the shadow of the House of Representatives to become a dynamic

United States Senate, A.D. 1850

legislative body. In this Chamber, it shaped a tradition of unlimited debate, attracted orators and statesmen, and reenforced senatorial prerogatives in battles with successive presidents over the direction of the nation's economy.

The Senate's outstanding orators and statesmen, many recruited from the House of Representatives, included three who articulated the growing nation's regional tensions. The legendary orator Daniel Webster of Massachusetts spoke for an industrializing New England in the context of a strong national union. The "Great Compromiser," Kentucky's Henry Clay, represented the western frontier and called for government funding of roads, canals, and other internal improvements. John C. Calhoun of South Carolina defended states' rights and slavery to the point of insisting that states could nullify federal laws. Alternately feuding and cooperating, these men forged the legislative compromises that preserved the Union in the decades before the Civil War. Today, members occasionally return to the Old Chamber to reflect on what it means to be a senator of the United States.

George Washington's Farewell Address. Each February, the Senate performs its oldest non-legislative ritual. This 45-minute event consists of one senator reading President George Washington's 1796 Farewell Address in open session. In these remarks, Washington warned that the forces of geographical sectionalism, political factionalism, and interference by foreign powers in the nation's domestic affairs threatened the stability of the Republic. He urged Americans to put aside sectional jealousies to pursue common national interests.

In January 1862, with the Constitution endangered by the Civil War, citizens

of Philadelphia petitioned Congress to celebrate the forthcoming 130th anniversary of Washington's birth by reading his classic address in one of its chambers. On

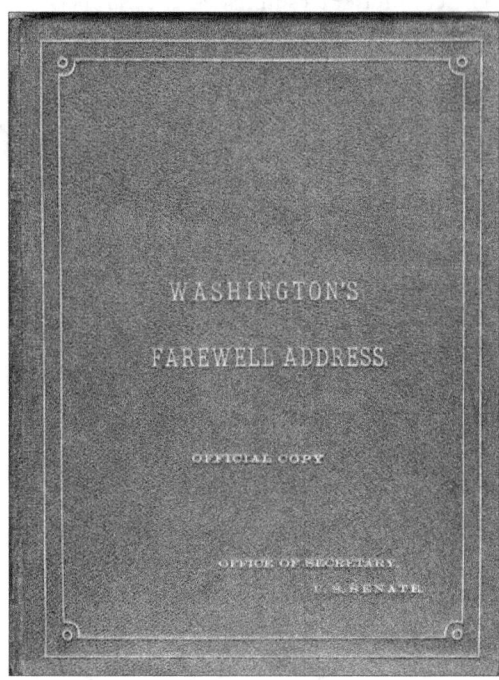

Washington's Farewell Address inscription book

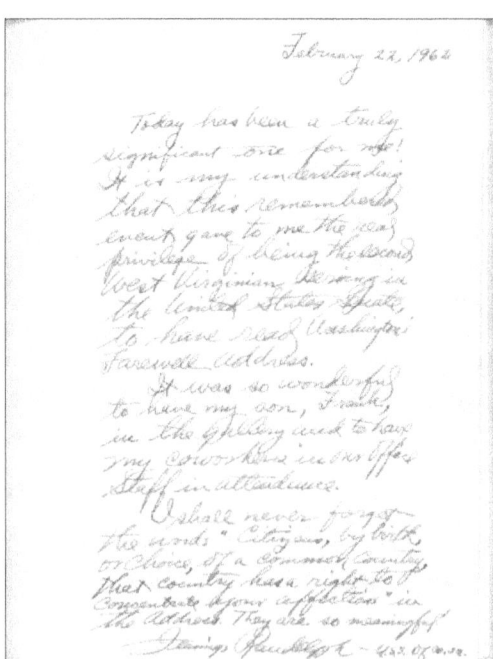

Inscription page of Senator Jennings Randolph, D–WV

February 22, 1862, both bodies gathered in the House Chamber to hear Secretary of the Senate John Forney perform that duty. Since 1896, the Senate has observed Washington's Birthday each year with a senator delivering the Farewell Address. Members and gallery visitors receive a booklet containing a historical account of the address and its text. At the conclusion of each reading, the appointed senator inscribes his or her name and brief comments in a black, leather-bound book, first used on February 22, 1900. That member also receives a framed certificate of appointment signed by the vice president and authenticated with Senate seal and ribbon.

Senate spouses' organization. In the 18th and 19th centuries, members often traveled to the nation's capital without their wives and families. Trying to live and work out of cramped rooms in a nearby boardinghouse often proved difficult. One example in the House of Representatives was Abraham Lincoln, whose wife Mary and their three small children moved with him to Washington in 1847. Crowded conditions, however, soon convinced Lincoln to send his family to Mary's parents' home in Kentucky for the balance of his single term in Congress. In the 20th century, improved transportation and year-round congressional sessions inspired many members—contrary to Lincoln's experience—to move their families to second homes in the Washington area.

In 1917, as the United States entered World War I, several among the growing number of resident spouses established the "Ladies of the Senate" to provide a sociable organization devoted to community service. Known informally as the "Wives' Club,"

Senate wives' Red Cross chapter meeting, 1959

Senate spouses met in a basement room of the Russell Senate Office Building to knit, sew, and roll bandages for the Red Cross. Today, renamed the "Senate Spouses," they still operate as a Red Cross chapter. Senator Elizabeth Dole, a former Senate spouse, once headed the American Red Cross.

Modern-era Senate spouses, actively engaged in their own careers, enjoy organizing an annual luncheon to honor the First Lady. This tradition dates from 1942 when First Lady Eleanor Roosevelt dropped by for lunch with the "Ladies of the Senate"—bringing her own sandwich in a bag. Today, the organization, whose members include a former president of the United States and former Senate majority leader, provides a gala luncheon for all attendees.

End-of-session valedictories and eulogies. A well-established ritual occurs near the end of each biennial session of Congress. Members deliver floor speeches to honor colleagues who will not be returning for the next Congress. For senior members, those remarks extend through many pages of the *Congressional Record* and in some instances are subsequently published as Senate documents. In the session's final moments, the two party floor leaders commend one another, thank floor and committee staffs for their long hours and tireless effort, and then telephone the president to inquire whether he has any more business for Congress before it adjourns for the year. In recent times, the Senate has sponsored a "retirement dinner" to honor departing members.

Funerals and memorial services. As a relatively small and traditionally collegial body, the Senate actively mourns the death of an incumbent member. Today, thanks to improved health care, fewer senators die in office than was the case prior to the mid-1960s. Consequently, there is no longer much need for the elaborate system of Senate funeral rituals that had developed during the 19th and early 20th centuries.

In those earlier times, several incumbent senators died each year. For senators who succumbed while Congress was in session, the Senate adjourned the following day's proceedings in that member's memory, conducted funerals or memorial services in its Chamber—with a large floral tribute resting on the deceased member's vacant desk and black crepe covering the chair—sent delegations of senators to accompany the remains back home, and authorized members to wear black armbands for 30 days. For those senators who died during an extended adjournment period, the Senate, upon reconvening, conducted a collective memorial service in its Chamber with appropriate prayers and musical tributes.

Today's Senate funeral and memorial traditions for incumbent senators reflect that earlier experience. The Senate still adjourns the day's session in memory of the deceased member, sends delegations to the funeral—with members departing from and returning to the Capitol on the same day thanks to modern high-speed transportation—and sets aside a portion of a day's schedule for memorial tributes. Such tributes appear as part of the official record of floor proceedings. Many are

Funeral of Majority Leader Joseph Robinson, 1937

subsequently collected along with news obituaries and other pertinent documents to be issued as an official Senate publication. The American flag is flown at half-staff on the day of the incumbent's death and the following day.

Senator Claude Pepper, D–FL, later in his 53-year congressional career

"CITADEL OF CONSTITUTIONAL AND DEMOCRATIC LIBERTIES"

Elected to the Senate in 1936, Florida's Claude Pepper emerged as one of the stars of his freshman class. In 1939, the editors of the *Harvard Law Review* considered this thoughtful member, and Harvard Law School graduate, to be the ideal person to review an important new book on the Senate. *The Senate of the United States,* by Professor George Haynes, is today considered the first comprehensive scholarly history of the Senate and its procedures. Senator Pepper gladly completed his assigned review. In a key paragraph, he offered a statement that memorably captures his initial impressions as a new member of the United States Senate.

The varied and extraordinary functions and powers of the Senate make it, according to one's point of view, a hydra-headed monster or the citadel of constitutional and democratic liberties. Like democracy itself, the Senate is inefficient, unwieldy, inconsistent; it has its foibles, its vanities, its members who are great, the near great, and those who think they are great. But like democracy also, it is strong, it is sound at the core, it has survived many changes, it has saved the country many catastrophes, it is a safeguard against any form of tyranny, good or bad, which consciously or unconsciously might tend to remove the course of government from persistent public scrutiny. In the last analysis, it is probably the price we in America have to pay for liberty.

For further information

Senate Web site: www.senate.gov
("Art and History")

U.S. Congress. Senate. *The Senate, 1789–1989,* by Senator Robert C. Byrd. S. Doc. 100–20, 100th Congress, 1st sess., 4 volumes, 1988–1994.

_____. *Senate Historical Almanac,* by Senator Bob Dole. S. Doc. 100–35, 100th Congress, 2d sess., 1989.

_____. *United States Senate Catalogue of Fine Art,* by William Kloss and Diane Skvarla. S. Doc. 107–11, 107th Congress, 2d sess., 2002.

_____. *United States Senate Catalogue of Graphic Art,* essays by Diane K. Skvarla and Donald A. Ritchie. S. Doc. 109–2, 109th Congress, 1st sess., 2005.

_____. *200 Notable Days: Senate Stories, 1787 to 2002,* by Richard A. Baker. S. Pub 109–22, 109th Congress, 2d sess., 2006.

Image Credits